Faithful
PAPER
CRAFTING

Notecards, Gift Tags, Scrapbook Paper & More To Share The Blessing

ROBIN PICKENS

DESIGN ORIGINALS
an Imprint of Fox Chapel Publishing
www.d-originals.com

Welcome

to a wealth of faith papercrafting!

This book provides you with ready-made papercrafting materials that will add a pop of pure beauty to your home, your gifts, and your spirit. However, the extra-special thing about the crafting elements in this book is that although they're beautiful as standalone pieces, they also offer a ton of flexibility to add your own personal, inspired touches! You can use your own words, embellish with other crafting materials, and combine cards with scrapbook paper designs to create beautiful pieces. Pick the color schemes you like and the sentiments that speak to you, and let the creativity flow!

Project Ideas

Crafting Materials

CRAFTED CARDS

Craft a heartfelt card for any recipient or occasion by pulling your favorite art cards from this book and adding all kinds of fun embellishments. Layer with scrapbook papers, add gemstones and glitter, use 3-dimensional glue dots to add some height to your card… the possibilities are endless when sending sentiments and sunshine to everyone you know!

The art cards and accompanying scrapbook paper cards in this book come in a variety of sizes and backings. You can cut the border off of the smaller art cards and mount the art on top of a scrapbook paper card so that it creates a new border; you can paste a scrapbook paper card to the back of an art card back to back and write your own sentiment on the colored side; or you can simply embellish an existing art card and give it to a friend. Experiment with different combinations!

Burst forth in
Beauty
& Radiant
Love

and the greatest of these is L

Blessed

"The Lord bless you and keep you, the
Lord make his face shine on you and be
gracious to you; the Lord turn His face
toward you and give you peace."
—Numbers 6:24–26

Notice
the
beauty
in the
tiniest
deta

*Don't forget
to check out the
colorable cards
on pages 55-60 as well
as the ready-to-roll
foldable cards
on pages 49-54!*

Pray

The large envelope on page 79 is a standard size and should be happily accepted and mailed at your local post office.

CRAFTED ENVELOPES

The envelope is a very important facet of card giving, so why settle for plain, uninspired envelopes when you could have completely personalized, prettily patterned homes for your cards to travel in? Before you start, remove the envelope templates on pages 77–80. Laminate the templates or paste them to thick poster board to ensure your templates live a long, healthy life of envelope shaping.

How to Assemble an Envelope

1. Trace your master envelope template onto your favorite piece of double-sided scrapbook paper (see pages 77–80). Cut out the newly traced template and set your master template aside.

2. Referring to the dashed lines on your master template, create the shape of the envelope by first folding the two side flaps in toward the center, then folding in the bottom flap. Double check the way you're folding so your favorite scrapbook pattern is on the outside of the envelope and the accent color is on the inside.

3. Tape the bottom three folded flaps of the envelope together, leaving the top flap free to open and close. If you plan to hand deliver your envelope to its recipient, feel free to only tape on the inside, where the tape will be hidden. If you want to mail your crafted envelope, add extra tape on the outside seams of the flaps to ensure that the envelope doesn't come open in transit.

4. Insert your completed card, add your destination to the front in some fancy script, stick on a stamp, and off it goes!

CRAFTED GIFT TAGS

Like envelopes, gift tags are essential to gift giving. How else are we supposed to identify which perfectly wrapped parcel goes to which perfectly picked friend? In this book you will find 16 gift tags (see pages 69–72) ready to be cut out, crafted up, and sent packing.

Just like the cards, these gift tags are lovely enough to stand alone but can become mini masterpieces with just a few added elements. The same ribbons, gemstones, and layered effects you can use to make cards can be used for the tags to create the most magnificent gift set.

Don't be afraid to embellish! Add hand lettering and bling, or even tie a cute charm to a gift tag.

Ali

for you

be joyful

Fill my heart with joy

Faith, Hope and Love

GOD IS LOVE

◖ 1 JOHN 4:16 ◗

BELIEVE

HOPE

PRAY

FORGIVE

COMFORT

LOVE

REJOICE

CRAFTED BOOKMARKS

Reading scripture is a serious endeavor, and we all know how frustrating it can be to lose your spot. Ensure this never happens by keeping a lovely, inspirational bookmark between the pages of your Bible. Add a personal touch to your bookmarks by including notes on the back of them, and then, perhaps, by making your own tassels!

How to Make a Mini Tassel

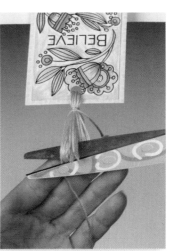

1. Punch a hole in the bookmark. Wrap your chosen yarn/twine/embroidery floss evenly and snugly around the width of your palm.

2. Slide the wrapped bundle off of your palm, keeping it flat and intact. Thread the bundle through the hole, then fold it to bring the two halves together.

3. Tie a piece of yarn tightly around the entire bundle, right at the edge of the bookmark. You can wrap the piece of yarn around the bundle multiple times before tying it.

4. Cut the top of all the loops to create the fringe. Fluff the fringe and trim it as desired, being sure to also trim the piece of yarn used to tie the bundle.

Trust in the Lord without wavering
—Psalm 26:1

Always be joyful
—1 Thessalonians 5:16

Glory to God
—Luke 2:14

Every good and perfect gift is from above
—James 1:17

Fill my heart with joy
—Psalm 4:7

CRAFTED MINI CARDS

In this book you will find a collection of mini cards that have been beautifully illustrated with faithful imagery and inspiring sentiments. Laminate them for your wallet or to slip to a friend in time of need, or perhaps make some DIY fridge magnets with them! You never know when you will need a little pick-me-up to get through the day, and these mini cards are a perfect reminder that you're not alone in your journey. If you don't have a laminator, use clear packing tape to laminate your mini cards right at home with little to no fuss.

Praise God, trust God, thank God

Let your light shine
—Matthew 5:16

How to Make a Fridge Magnet

1. Collect your materials. You will need your favorite mini cards from this book, a few sheets of mat board, glue, adhesive magnets (dots or strips), a container of Mod Podge Dimensional Magic Glaze or similar product, and a container of regular Mod Podge decoupage medium (matte or glossy) or similar product.

2. Cut the mat board to the size you want your magnet. Cut out and glue a piece of scrapbook paper to the mat board, ensuring that all of the corners are completely adhered. Glue a mini card on top of the scrapbook paper.

3. Use the decoupage medium to cover the entire face of the magnet, starting with the outside perimeter and filling in*. Use the glaze to accent select areas of the mini card. Use a straight pin or safety pin to pop any bubbles that may form in the glaze. (Putting glaze all over the entire magnet may cause it to warp.)

4. After the glaze has dried completely, attach your magnets to the reverse side. Voilà: you are on your way to transforming your fridge into a spiritual mood board!

*Sealing your entire magnet with decoupage medium is a good idea because it helps protect your magnet from fridge spills and makes it more durable for repeatedly taking it off the fridge to pin new things.

CRAFTED FRAMEABLES

One of the most popular, classic, and effortless ways to fill your home with a faithful spirit is with framed inspirational art. Placing a beautifully colored picture or divine quote in an eye-catching frame will always be a genuine way to spread love, whether it's for your home or a gift for a loved one. Take it one step further by jazzing up your frame with embellishments like stickers, ribbons, or hand lettering.

Be
JOYFUL
in hope.
PATIENT
in affliction.
FAITHFUL
in prayer.

ROMANS 12:12

Let your
light shine
Matthew 5:16

Ready, Set, Craft!

On the following pages you'll find everything you need to make gorgeous crafts—perforated, colored, and all ready for you! Just go for it and don't stress about whether you're doing it "right." Pour your soul into your work, and the result will be beautiful! Enjoy!

_____
_____
_____
_____
_____

He has made everything beautiful in its time.
—Ecclesiastes 3:11

He has made everything beautiful in its time.
—Ecclesiastes 3:11

_____
_____
_____
_____
_____

_____

_____

_____

_____

_____

You make the dawn
and the sunset shout for joy.
—Psalm 65:8b

_____

_____

_____

_____

_____

You make the dawn
and the sunset shout for joy.
—Psalm 65:8b

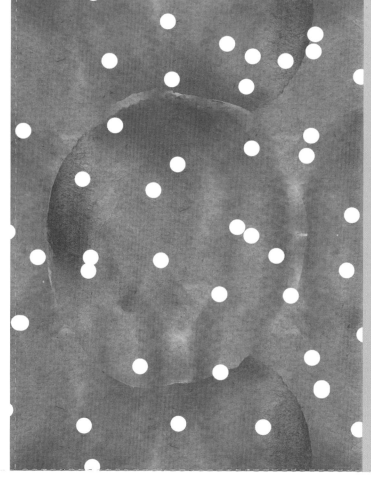

_____
_____
_____
_____
_____

Nothing will be impossible with God.
—Luke 1:37

_____
_____
_____
_____
_____

Nothing will be impossible with God.
—Luke 1:37

_____

_____

_____

_____

_____

She is clothed with strength and dignity
and she laughs without fear of the future.
—Proverbs 31:25

_____

_____

_____

_____

_____

She is clothed with strength and dignity
and she laughs without fear of the future.
—Proverbs 31:25

with God
all things
are possible.

MATTHEW 19:26

with God
all things
are possible.

MATTHEW 19:26

"For I know the plans I have for you," declares the LORD,
"plans to prosper you and not to harm you, plans to
give you hope and a future."
—Jeremiah 29:11

"For I know the plans I have for you," declares the LORD,
"plans to prosper you and not to harm you, plans to
give you hope and a future."
—Jeremiah 29:11

find Strength in
faith &
family

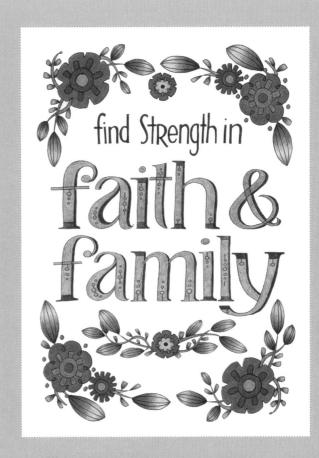

find Strength in
faith &
family

_____
_____
_____
_____
_____

*As for me and my house,
we will serve the LORD.
—Joshua 24:15*

_____
_____
_____
_____
_____

*As for me and my house,
we will serve the LORD.
—Joshua 24:15*

_____

_____

_____

_____

_____

*"The LORD bless you and keep you; the
LORD make his face shine on you and be
gracious to you; the LORD turn his face
toward you and give you peace."*
—Numbers 6:24–26

_____

_____

_____

_____

_____

*"The LORD bless you and keep you; the
LORD make his face shine on you and be
gracious to you; the LORD turn his face
toward you and give you peace."*
—Numbers 6:24–26

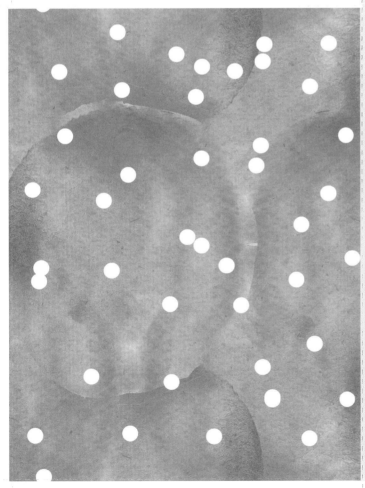

These three remain: faith, hope, and love.
But the greatest of these is love.
—1 Corinthians 13:13

These three remain: faith, hope, and love.
But the greatest of these is love.
—1 Corinthians 13:13

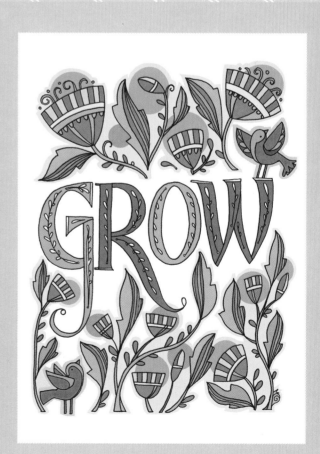

*"The kingdom of heaven is like a mustard seed....
Though it is the smallest of all seeds, yet when it
grows it is the largest of garden plants."
—Matthew 13:31, 32*

*"The kingdom of heaven is like a mustard seed....
Though it is the smallest of all seeds, yet when it
grows it is the largest of garden plants."
—Matthew 13:31, 32*

_____
_____
_____
_____
_____

Be kind and compassionate to one another,
forgiving each other, just as in Christ
God forgave you.
—Ephesians 4:32

_____
_____
_____
_____
_____

Be kind and compassionate to one another,
forgiving each other, just as in Christ
God forgave you.
—Ephesians 4:32

_____

_____

_____

_____

_____

Love the LORD your God with all your heart and
with all your soul and with all your strength.
—Deuteronomy 6:5

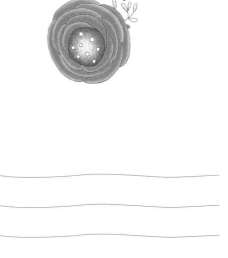

_____

_____

_____

_____

_____

Love the LORD your God with all your heart and
with all your soul and with all your strength.
—Deuteronomy 6:5

Let all that you do
be done in
LOVE

Let all that you do
be done in
LOVE

Love bears all things, believes all things, hopes all things, endures all things.
—1 Corinthians 13:7

Love bears all things, believes all things, hopes all things, endures all things.
—1 Corinthians 13:7

_____
_____
_____
_____
_____

*Do not be anxious about anything, but in
every situation, by prayer and petition, with
thanksgiving, present your requests to God.*
—Philippians 4:6

_____
_____
_____
_____
_____

*Do not be anxious about anything, but in
every situation, by prayer and petition, with
thanksgiving, present your requests to God.*
—Philippians 4:6

_____

_____

_____

_____

_____

Praise God from whom all blessings flow; Praise Him, all creatures here below; Praise Him above, ye heavenly host; Praise Father, Son, and Holy Ghost. Amen.
—Thomas Ken

_____

_____

_____

_____

_____

Praise God from whom all blessings flow; Praise Him, all creatures here below; Praise Him above, ye heavenly host; Praise Father, Son, and Holy Ghost. Amen.
—Thomas Ken

_____
_____
_____
_____
_____

My cup overflows with blessings.
—Psalm 23:5

_____
_____
_____
_____
_____

My cup overflows with blessings.
—Psalm 23:5

...and the greatest of these is Love

1 CORINTHIANS 13:13

...and the greatest of these is Love

1 CORINTHIANS 13:13

Be devoted to one another in love.
Honor one another above yourselves.
—Romans 12:10

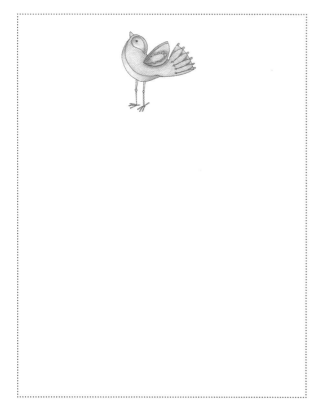

Be devoted to one another in love.
Honor one another above yourselves.
—Romans 12:10

Just remove these two ready-to-roll cards and fold them down the middle!

This is the day that the Lord has made;
let us rejoice and be glad in it.
—Psalm 118:24

Just remove these two ready-to-roll cards and fold them down the middle!

_____
_____
_____
_____
_____

_____
_____
_____
_____
_____

"For where two or three gather in my name,
there am I with them."
—Matthew 18:20

Just remove these two ready-to-roll cards and fold them down the middle!

Hope anchors the soul.
—Hebrews 6:19

Let your creativity loose with these colorable cards!

Fear not, for I am with you.
—Isaiah 41:10

For we walk by faith, not by sight.
—2 Corinthians 5:7

_____

_____

_____

_____

_____

Fear not, for I am with you.
—Isaiah 41:10

For we walk by faith, not by sight.
—2 Corinthians 5:7

Let your creativity loose with these colorable cards!

We love because He first loved us.
—1 John 4:19

The joy of the LORD is your strength.
—Nehemiah 8:10

We love because He first loved us.
—1 John 4:19

The joy of the LORD is your strength.
—Nehemiah 8:10

Let your creativity loose with these colorable cards!

"My command is this:
Love each other as I have loved you."
—John 15:12

Of all earthly music, that which
reaches farthest into heaven is the
beating of a truly loving heart.
—Henry Ward Beecher

"My command is this:
Love each other as I have loved you."
—John 15:12

Of all earthly music, that which
reaches farthest into heaven is the
beating of a truly loving heart.
—Henry Ward Beecher

Be
JOYFUL
in hope,
PATIENT
in affliction,
FAITHFUL
in prayer.

ROMANS 12:12

Praise God,
trust God,
thank God

Let your
light shine

—Matthew 5:16

Glory
to God

—Luke 2:14

Fill my
heart
with joy

—Psalm 4:7

Trust in
the LORD
without
wavering

—Psalm 26:1

Amen

Cling to that
which is good

—Romans 12:9

All things
work together
for good

—Romans 8:28

Every good
and perfect
gift is
from above

—James 1:17

Be
strong
and
courageous

—Deuteronomy 31:6

Count it
all joy

—James 1:2

Give thanks
in all
circumstances

—1 Thessalonians 5:18

Seek first
the kingdom
of God

—Matthew 6:33

It is
well
with
my soul

—Horatio G. Spafford

Always
be
joyful

—1 Thessalonians 5:16

Seek
peace
and
pursue it

—Psalm 34:14

Rise up
and pray

—Luke 22:46

I will
sustain
you

—Isaiah 46:4

BELIEVE

HOPE

PRAY

FORGIVE

COMFORT

LOVE

REJOICE

Glory to God

Faith, Hope and Love

PRAY

GOD IS LOVE

1 JOHN 4:16

Small Envelope Template - <small>Cut out, trace, and reuse. Folding instructions on page 7.</small>

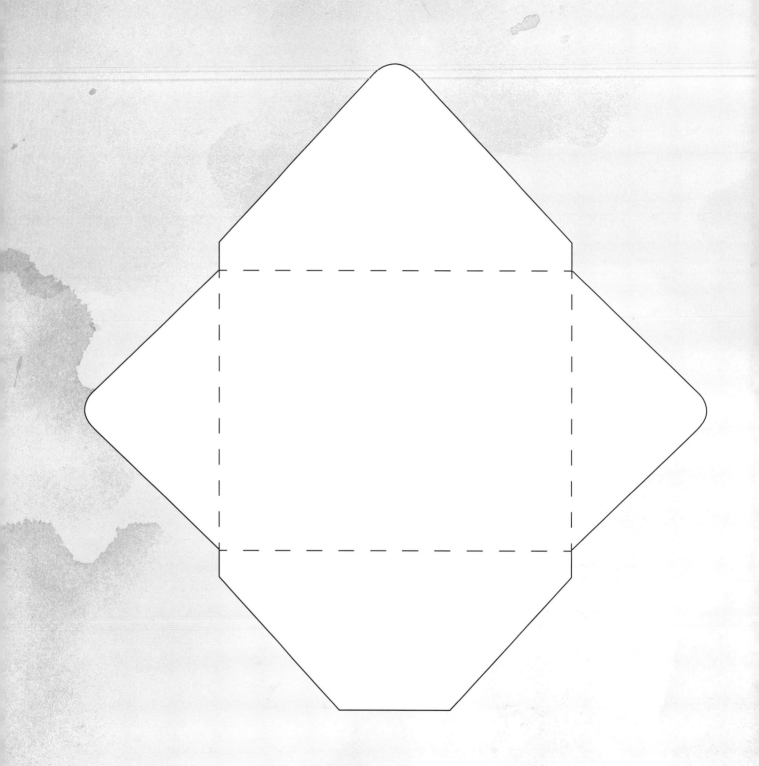

Large Envelope Template - Cut out, trace, and reuse. Folding instructions on page 7.